GLIDE

GLIDE

Louise Crisp

PUNCHER & WATTMANN

First published in 2021
Published by Puncher and Wattmann
PO Box 279
Waratah NSW 2298

http://www.puncherandwattmann.com
puncherandwattmann@bigpond.com

NATIONAL
LIBRARY
OF AUSTRALIA

A catalogue entry for this book is available from the National Library of Australia.

ISBN   9781925780857

Cover design by David Musgrave
Typesetting by Morgan Arnett
Printed by Lightning Source International

This project has been assisted by the Australian Government through the Australia Council, its arts funding and advisory body.

Australian Government

Australia Council for the Arts

Contents

PART ONE
GLIDE

(Yellow-bellied Glider *Petaurus australis*)

Phenology
(Mt Alfred State Forest, East Gippsland)

Nectar

Stands of eucalypts prefer to flower together
Older trees bear more flowers
Large-flower tree species
like Ironbark
proffer
pendulous
the pale light
of large flowers
At night they open
more profusely and
the rim of nectar fills
hanging upside down suspended

The only way to obtain the bounteous
sweet fluid is to dip one's tongue inside
The flora-mammal mutualism: taking pollen
on snouts across country to a distant stand of Ironbark

Sap

The sweetest tree is the scraggliest:
Apple Box —
        sweet tooth sweet apple sweet apple-box sap
                sweet incision:
rough barked but desirable

Disregarded tree of the lowland
forests: scraggly
useless for the utilitarian settler logging, burning, fencing

Its sweet groves harbour
supplicant gliders

Flow

Testing the tree:
swift flows the sap –
       fresh feed marks in early summer
The yellow inner bark scored up the
smooth trunk of Mountain Grey Gum
Notches flash intermittently
bright in the sunlight
Driving through foothill forest
the locus of choice
is startling
in its rarity

Patchiness

1.
At older sites
gliders re-appear
as the harvest is re-instigated
Sap –
old feed trees they come
back to
dispersed along
ridges & mid-slopes
The riskiest aspect:

reliance on perpetuity
in a logging forest

2.
Nectar, honeydew, manna –
succession
becomes unreliable
Large gaps open
as the forest is felled
patchiness is exacerbated
Seasonal elements
entice the eucalypts
to flower
In response
the provocation blossoms
as months of hunger

Decorticating
Splitting the bark ribbons

Emergent above rainforest
in Flaggy Creek valley

a flush of russet in autumn:
peeling the decorticating –

They opened the hanging
rolls of dead bark and

even hung by their hind legs
to unravel the bark:

foraging for arthropods
on Mountain Grey Gum

The crunch of protein
abundant at bark shed

coincides with last milk
and first foraging

Among the upper branches
newly independent offspring

twirl & peel & un-ribbon

Woodcut

Pearls & berries
golden orange
in clusters
An intricate pattern
up the smooth
grey & white
trunk of the Mountain
Grey gum:
fresh feed marks

Coupe 735-518-0008
(Wattle Ck Rd)

Eyes closed
faces, lips & mouths –
so many creatures
engraved one above
the other –
a history
of inhabitation

SPZ 821 planned burn
(Wattle Ck Tk)

The head of a person
weeping
dark sap
shoulders
Half ring-barked
Apple Box tree
opposite
a coupe
of young
Silvertop

(Harding Rd)

A diagonal sword
scar
a long tear
The healing fold
of bark
occludes
the wound
Claws & teeth
tend to sap
The scar lengthens

Coupe 735-520-0015
(Watts Ck Tk)

Diagonals
& diamonds
cross-hatched
bark calluses
overlain by more
recent incisions —
recurrent
visitation:
provident *bridgesiana*

North of clear fell
(Harding Rd)

Apple Box trees
on a bend
in the track
the deep mouth
makes a heart
Glider language —
intimate locality

Coupe 735-520-0013,
(Watts Ck)

Reddish kino
shredded bark
intensively harvested
big old Messmate
Drying sap
a stain
of black diesel
opposite VicForests'
illegal rainforest logging

Coupe 832-502-0017
(Puggaree Rd)

Abandoned school
abandoned tree
old sign:
black *V*s
glide further
up the road
Selected tree
tall ladder
horizontal steps
a fresh pattern
tan paw marks

Coupe 737-505-0001
(Melwood School Rd)

Three hundred year-old tree
generations
of gliders
have fed upon
the Mountain
Grey Gum standing
beside the headwaters
of Bendoc River
under the conical hill
scheduled for logging

Coupe 892-502-0012
(off Mustards Tk)

Sap waterfall
falls 15 metres
to the ground
Old Mountain
Grey Gum
unlogged gully
narrow remnant
gliders are now
compelled
to prevail in

Coupe 735-510-0018
(Rain Gauge Tk)

A veil sways
sideways
across the Mountain
Grey Gum
Kill Me Dead Ck
is lively with birds
Rufous Fantails
Yellow-tufted Honeyeaters
Gang Gangs
White Cockatoos
& Lyrebirds
Upstream an unknown
voice calls *Heelp*

Mt Alfred-
Kill Me Dead planned burn
(Kill Me Dead Tk)

Twin-stemmed
Apple Box tree
on the dry ridge
above Flaggy Ck
Burnt & re-burnt
parsimonious understorey

(Melwood Boundary Tk)

A flight
Of arrowheads

An arm   Coupe 735-520-0010
around the trunk   (Lamble Tk)
clasps
the Apple Box tree:
goanna
or glider
the lineage
carves itself
into bark —
forest entreaty

Patagium

The full moon rises over the shadows of the half-empty forest of the
    foothills cold & clear
coming down to bare paddocks through open woodland the moonlight
    catches up behind
Walking into a cacophony of Yellow-bellied Gliders and Sugar Gliders
    in the floral abundance
of young Ironbark trees hard against the fence at the edge of the track
    refugees of the logging
I gasp at the astonishing reveal of yellow furred belly edged with black
    as a glider takes off
above me patagium open wide as the plateau covering my head all our
    arms open too we cry
an unknown prayer for all the forest species daily destroyed nightly we
    revisit to encounter

Patagium: gliding membrane.

Flight paths
Blind as a colonial

I. Roaring Mag
A glide between two knolls on Roaring Mag Ridge above the Mitchell —
swooping through White Stringybark, Ironbark and Silvertop 30 degrees
to the horizontal and considerable manoeuvrability turning 180 degrees
in mid air from the fifth finger to the ankle across country 100m at a time
to the Apple Box sap-feed trees on Baldhills Track scheduled for burning
Warm evening in summer a light breeze sufficient to stir leaves at midnight

2. Watts Creek
A glider road travels east-west across the low plateau of the foothills
from the remnant patch of bush on private land to the rough track
between tributaries of Watts Creek the last stand of old hollow trees
hosting dens to thread through young forest picked over 50 years ago
to the grove of Apple Box trees windward the cold wind in winter
is turned aside by the rising land & furrowed Ironbarks along the border

3. Wattle Creek
A network of glide paths on the western fall down to Wattle Creek
from the knoll on Harding Road the deeply scored Apple Box sap trees
are red with frequent use and almost dying from the encircling incisions
Gentled by unburnt open country Rusty Velvet-bush and *Pomaderris* near
to flower I cross diagonal towards the sap trees at the washed out ford
the escarpment chittering with swift parrots in the flowering Red Box

4. Stony Creek
Flogged and *hammered* the lowland forest for decades repeatedly
burned and logged the narrow verdant strip along Stony Creek
a haven for Wonga Pigeon, Whipbirds and Tufted Honeyeaters
tall Mountain Grey Gums shade the sandstone slabs & shallow pools
Above the creek flat a few Apple Box sap-feed trees gather in a village
of gliders approached via a flight path un-countenanced before any burn

5. Harding Track

The scars on the Apple Box tree on the hill are grey and calloused over
within a glide of the old-growth forest along Stony Creek clear-felled
to the edge of water – Harding Track runs east past stumps wide enough
to stand two men legs apart to balance a chainsaw against the slope
Oval shadows mark the entry to hollows in two Mountain Grey Gums
left standing beside the track the rest of the hillside is silenced voiding
the flight path uphill from here – never to make it back to the ridgeline

Call
(Mitchell River National Park)

Whirring in darkness the young glider
through stringybark and wattle maintains
a trajectory to the grove
of Apple Box

along the curve of the ridge the adults
shepherd & gurgle – on the outlands:
the border of the home
range, call

to locate kin at a distance; gather
& harbour
in the flowering Ironbarks
Here – directional co-ordination

(intra-family)
& exclusive territory announced
on a rising cadence
an intense single or double shriek

whilst foraging or landing on a tree trunk
loud enough to be heard at 400 metres
or ultra-sonic: outside the range
of humanity?

(Greater Glider *Petauroides volans*)

Whaling
(Mt Alfred State Forest, East Gippsland)

1.
A forty year rotation: the back of a whale
flensing the hillside —
carved up into blocks cubes of
old forest
clear-felled:
coupes back-to-back for kilometres across
the catchment of Stony Creek to the headwaters

Up under Mt Alfred the tall standing forest abuts
another coupe of young Silvertop
A network of filaments
runs underground
searching for solicitude, absent companions
(stems of Weeping Grass)
An exposed skeleton, shoulder blade, wing bone
ribs of the land
fold into the valley to the west

The lowered horizon, careful
not to move
beneath the falling tree the
glider abandons its den for the canopy
of the next tall tree climbing
before it is felled
A long glide
paws to chin
into low wattle branches
Starkly black & white or creamy-grey

against the sky
Wandering clumsily its flattened
territory, picked up at night
in the yellow eyes
of a Powerful Owl —
stripped & torn

Headless

2.
Turned aside from the warm density
of Musk Gully rainforest
VicForests' heavy machinery extends
along a chain of coupes on the western fall
A monoculture of *Eucalyptus sieberi*
replaces the foothill forest:
old trees of Mountain Grey Gum
Apple Box, Ironbark, Red Box
Stringybarks & Gippsland
Blue Gum
with its complicated understory
all the way to the Mitchell River
For Greater Gliders
in a scrap of home range
hungry
in a plantation of Silvertop
unpalatable means sacrificial

Horizontal

loving the horizontal —
the rough furred White Stringybark
branch underside bark reddened and
smoothed by the winding and
unwinding of the Greater Glider's long
tail during its night-time pose stationary on
the divide above Watts Creek a contiguous linear patch of giant
old Mountain Grey Gums replicated in staged locations to
the south, southerly, southernmost, downstream to farmland;
to the north: the abandoned logging lands of Stony Creek —
(entwined it curls over the branch to look down at us)

II
walking the interconnecting
                    horizontal branches of adjacent trees
travelling the canopy in the deep gully of Wattle Creek —
          Manna Gum, River Peppermint and Grey Gums: a pre-determined
                    route
via a minimum number of trees from the den to reach
          the desired
                    feed trees *involving the occasional leap*

III
two appear against the sky above the dead stag
black & white and grey & white from the hollow

as the half moon disappears behind cloud
on Unnamed Track we relocate the black & white

glider the following night higher still & paused
ascending the straight stem of a Messmate

its long bushy black tail brushing softly
against the solidity of the tall tree trunk

IV
The Giant Burrowing Frog carries the huge trees on its back: rarity of eggs
In Watts Creek east branch a frog's call ensures the emergence of gliders

V
The Greater Glider's eyes gleam brilliantly from its stringybark branch
    above the ford
on Watts Creek west as I watch with the spotlight it descends from the
    horizontal — behold
a long creamy tail carried upright as it climbs headfirst down the trunk
    verticals of light
Through leaves lowered the tail swings down behind it feathery: the
    glider turns into dark

Home range

Strong as attachment
fatal as (VicForests)
belonging to its own
small home range

The glider's affinity
with its hollow bearing
den trees is woven into
the canopy of the night

sky: black leafy starless —
When felled becomes
extinction's trackless abyss:
an impossible migration

Calculation

Rope dancer:

      Territory <2ha

      Den Hollows: 4-18 each

      Den depth: >28cm

      Height of hollow entrance: 8-40m

Via a hollow branch

      Entrance diameter: 8-18cm

      Trees: DBH 54-200cm

      widely spaced in home range

Trees aged >120 years for hollows to form

      Only 1 out of every 3 trees with hollows is occupied

      Mid-storey shrubbery around den trees for cover from predators

VicForests:

Clear-felled coupes

Retain 4-5 habitat trees per ha (only if safe to do so)

Retain understorey and regrowth vegetation around each habitat tree

Protect habitat trees from regeneration burning

Burn after clear felling burn after clear felling burn after clear felling burn
Felled again in 40-85 years

***

From the ridge on 186 Track looking west into Stony Creek catchment
the poise of the dead blackened
habitat trees
standing outrageously above the regenerating Silvertop and White Stringybark
is not an effect of the silvery afternoon light

Elevation
(Unnamed Track, Watts Creek)

Twenty metres aloft
over the gradient of the hill slope

A long tail to steer by
& altering the curvature of the gliding

membrane either side
of the body: d
                  i
                  r
                  e
                  c
                  t
                  i
                  o
                  n
                  -al   changes

up to 90 degrees

Swoop, stall & extend
feet & claws to grasp the trunk

– scratch marks –

                  aerial again
                  ....

two toes to three in a pincer
g
r
i
p:

hold the high
upper branches of tall Grey Gums
Too knotty and hollow for logging
the last huge trees
in the steep gully:
host to silent inhabitants

Elevation is where Greater Gliders
choose to be − co-evolved with the old forest

the broad bendy canopy branches
of Mountain Grey Gums: embodied history

(Sugar Glider *Petaurus breviceps*)

Haulage
(Stoney Creek Rd coupes 735-510-0021 & -0022)

Jupiter rises as Venus sets
over Stony Creek valley
The stars are lower in the sky
over the newly clear-felled land

Three stars of the constellation
Orion hang down in stringybark
foliage to the north west
moving in a soft warm breeze

Alnitak, Alnilam, Mintaka
shimmer to distant voices:
a radio plays across the foothills
as hunters wave their spotlight

I walk towards the luminescent
wide-opened scar land to the north
a tiny Sugar Glider glides silently
across the opening – homing in

on a swift diagonal from the east
to a stringybark on the edge
of the logging road lightly tapping
the bark as it lands, scampers

up the tree trunk and disappears
further south into shadowy forest
Little stars, globes or eyes
are suspended beneath a branch

hanging out over the road
drops of sap glisten & spill
into dust /deeper in the trees
another Sugar Glider crosses

gliding through the beam
of light graceful as a visitation
Mopokes, tree creaks and Banjo
Frogs sounding beyond the haulage

Fireflies

1.

Late summer flickering through the foothill forest, alternating: brightly, fade
up along Flaggy Ck valley appearing & disappearing into distance fine misty
rain as the moon rises yipping at the edge of
dense brush of Black Wattle
The understorey
a harvest
of sap
in all seasons:
summer and autumn
gum setting to winter nodules
The distributed calls of Sugar Gliders
dependent on the density of *Acacia mearnsii*

2.

Sugar Gliders call as they move through the flowering stringybarks
below Mt Alfred; Lightwood, Sweet Bursaria and Blackwood
open in summer lowlands, along the ridge
the gliders escape the bright death
of a pursuing Sooty Owl
emerging from
rainforest
& up
over
the hill

a bomb
whistle
the
half
moon
frantic in the gully opposite Tabberabbera Track yerping for reassurance

3.
Curled up in a ball
in new leaves

gleaning manna
from the outer

foliage and buds
of an old Apple

Box tree rocking
in a tiny bunch

Its mate crouched
over a sap incision

in rough bark
along the top of

a horizontal branch
nose against the trunk

The gleaming pale
blue light of moonlight

on young Red Box
leaves glistens across

the plateau in clusters
sparse & iridescent

Distant glider calls
flare through the open

woodland in night's
starlit aural double

Windsucking
(Lake Tyers State Park)

Following the advancing flower

front as it opens sequentially

from the base of the inflorescence

Ascending the rich nectar bearing

spikes of Saw Banksia in groves

above the lake the Sugar Gliders

carry pollen about on fur & noses

In a summer of poor flowering

turn to chewing Blue Box for sap

white encrusting sugars can be seen

around the edges of the wound

of the rectangle of bark removed

from a tree above head height

of a wind sucking horse or in

autumn when the adjoining forest

unburnt for 60 years is put to flame

& all the flowering is sucked from the land

(Feathertail Glider *Acrobates pygmaeus*)

Ash

Too little to count

Falling like a leaf twirling
as the trees come down
at Bendoc in the thirties
hundreds of 'Pygmy
Flying Possums' abandon
their shredded bark nests

Half a dozen in a foothill
backyard flowering eucalypt
come to hand at midnight
in a flowering *Grevillea*
or fling past the head of a
woodcutter feeding his dogs

Climbing down the thin stem
of Blue Oliveberry in a grove
deep in a tributary gully as the
full moon rises over the ridge
body & fine feathered tail
silhouetted against the lit sky

Beside the track Sunshine Wattle
bursts into flower in the scant
lowland forest logged & repeatedly
burned: ash flutters into the rainforest
refuge cool and soothing below —
feather to the orange flame

(Squirrel Glider *Petaurus norfolcensis*)

Extinction
Its earthdom is the dream of finding itself
among all those absent ones (Eugenio Montejo)

Black back-stripe camouflage
in the Holocene forest at Murrindal

lugged into an Eastern Quoll's
den in the riverside karst formation

Carried by pre-colonial Sooty Owls
to a rock shelter roost on Friday Creek:

shadowy Milk Vine and Lillypillies
disguise the entrance under the cliff

Upstream the wide open grassy forest
extends across the low plateau above

the Mitchell River – northern limit
of the 'fertile' red gum plains, here

the ancient Red Gum, Red Box, Apple
Box, Blue Gum, Yellow Box & diverse

species of Stringybark we walk into
with a shock of recognition that this

is what has been destroyed across the
Gippsland Plains and foothills as each

succeeding generation of colonial forgets
another inventory of small marsupials

The scratch marks across the trunk of
the huge Red Gum on a dry billabong

near the stockyards on Rosevale Creek
may necessitate further nocturnal regard

Night Country
1. Mt Alfred - Sooty Owl gully

Night is another country
another language —
Listening to the sounds
of creatures reclaiming
the night forest, discreetly
The light of the full moon
throws a waterfall
of shadows off the ridge
into descending tiers
a hanging garden
      of foliage, vines
&
tendrils
         TALL
     Mountain Grey Gums
emergent above
the rainforest
amphitheatre
in deeper darkness
of the gully
From the ridgeline
of Mt Alfred
looking all the way out to the
Gippsland Lakes:
scratchings, branches
spring back, quiet rustlings
Boobook Owl and Sugar Glider
calls, whistles and ...
witness
indecipherable sounds
Heed —

gradually,   name
appearing
Listening intently
hours pass indivisibly
in the larger country
of the night

2. *Are you listening?*

Which squirrel is which?
In the five Gunaikurnai
dialects: words
for flying
squirrel, large flying
squirrel
great flying squirrel
& squirrel
(& flying mouse)
Recorded by missionaries
surveyors, anthropologists
and the
police
magistrate
in the 19th century
unaware of the 'taxonomic
subtleties'
of their interlocutors
& in the absence of
nocturnal auditory
encounters
Does the paucity of
vernacular names
written in English

skin-to-skin
disavow
the arboreal fauna
that persist with us?

PART TWO
BROLGA

Brolga

I.   (1840s)
Skulls rattle underwater
along Nuntin Creek
Ho, the Highland Brigade –
in their packed saddlebags
someone else's
birds & marshes

Parting reeds & rushes
cattle up to their bellies
in the fringing
freshwater swamps
that sweeten the Gippsland Lakes

devour the greeny cover
all the way
to the foothills

II
*Exploring the Gippsland Lakes
in 1882* tourists and sportsmen
sail down the La Trobe
'a fine broad stream'
on the steamer *Tanjil*
to cross Lake Wellington
en route to the Straits
& Bairnsdale with the
Lakes Navigation Company

On the northern shore
Strathfieldsaye homestead
is 'conspicuous'

on higher ground
64,000 acres occupied
by Odell Raymond in 1842
carrying 18,000 sheep & 1,000 cattle
coming down to drink
from the freshwater lake

A slope of Lightwood & Banksia
falls to a sandy shore
fanning east to Swell Point
beyond the hop gardens
a picnic ground for squatter families
to lounge on soft grasses
under 500 year-old Forest Red Gums
within a silent *cooee*
of Ramahyuck

III   (South West Victoria March 2015)
Gunning for ducks:
hunters arrive
en masse at dusk
on the eve of 'duck opening'
along the banks
of Bullrush Swamp

Flocking brolgas
abandon their roost
on Bullrush —
scarce expanse of water
persisting in drought
south of Gariwerd

Adjacent & dry:
the Minister declares

Krause Swamp
a waterbird refuge –
the flock of Brolgas
fruitlessly circles the sky

IV
George Curlewis 'took up' *The Heart*
in 1840 a run of 10 square miles

extending from the mouth
of the La Trobe River

The *heart of Gippsland*, a heart
in a tree, two hearts,

the heart shape of the land
where it joined the Morass

or marked on a ceremonial ground
below his homestead

After three years driven off
by warriors *numerous & hostile*

sold up to John Foster for 10 pounds
per year rent to the government

Ensuing action by Gippsland colonists –
the whitemen heart less

V   (1860s)
Mrs Eliza Montgomery
rode thirty miles across country
from *The Heart*

to Boisdale on the Avon
and not a fence did we see
until we came
to the Boisdale home paddock

We often passed flocks of
that most truly elegant bird
the native companion —

I have watched them, at sunset,
dancing together,
in a most graceful way,
gently waving their wings...
passing to and fro
as though following
out the figure of some dance.

Mr William Montgomery
applied to 'reclaim' the swamp
at Heart Morass for farmland
Within thirty years 5000 acres
of the Heart had been drained

Immediately the evolutions were over
the birds flew off
and I could never find out where to

VI
Pug hole pug hole the Herefords come down
from Glencoe's *fine uplands* at sunset
arched by the shadows of dead Red Gums

Over the fence bordering Dowd's Morass Reserve
a ransacked waterhole and thousands of hoof prints
Phragmites on this side lean frothily against wire

Deer hounds & a swivel gun enforced the order

VII
Lakeland boundaries: Tatungalung
canoes threading the Gippsland Lakes

VIII   (SW April 2015)
On the shore
of the lake
looking up –
pterosaurs
but more gentle
such long legs

A slow spiralling into clouds
three Brolgas
flying so high
they would see
any green soak surfacing
in the brown expanse of drought lands

An aerial map
of floating lagoons and marshes
now almost completely
erased by a scarified grid
of cropland road and farmland
living memory encounters as barren vacancy

IX   (SW 2015)
Brolgas evolved ever loved wetlands: a lost landscape
Freshwater shallow marshes nesting places drained
for grain and sheep
Un-homed, unmapped, dispersed to...

How to return
each year to the same shallow freshwater marsh
the adults for nesting
As interlinking marshes vanish from the land
the young chicks
emerge from their speckled shellnest circle of rushes
flightless for three months
each drying wetland now further then ever from another
Unprotected:
their hungry parents
forced to abandon them to fly further too far for food
Foxes slink in

X   (SW May 2015)
Chainsaws & trucks
on the SA border
felling operations
in a pine plantation
just beyond Ardno
the large flock of Brolgas
in swampy ground
nearby
has diminished
in recent days
to 25 birds
circulating the damp
hollow of a shallow
denuded wetland

A mob of sheep
graze along the bank
in line of sight
from the road
through fence wire
their legs entangle
in the bare paddock
Tentatively leaping
a male Brolga tosses
a blackened stick
or piece of cow dung
in the air:
the inedible surrogate
for a marshland tuber
fails to entice
his companion

XI   (SW May 2015)
Two Brolgas stroll
from the dam
by the roadside
honking
& trumpeting
out of sight
across the green paddock
on Kaldbro station
A deep wetland
planted with maize
recently harvested
A swift raptor silences
the White Cockatoos
screeching alarm
in a huge River Red Gum
Below me a great gathering

heads bowed
within the deep depression
of the old swamp
140 grey Brolgas
feeding on discarded grain
& maize stubble –
sweet abundance
generations once
were poisoned by

XII
Brolgas flourished in the splendid *evergreen*
morasses encompassing *the long waterholes*

and *deep slow waters* of the lowland rivers
spilling across the Gippsland Plains into the Lakes

I wander along levee banks in Dowd's Morass
looking for a colony of Spoonbills near open water

A line of dead Paperbarks in the distance
marks salt flooding in from Lake Wellington –

an ominous foreshadowing: the strata of reports
ineffectual against the increased speed of the tide

XIII   (SW Feb. 2016)
Flying close:
en famille, a formation
intercepted

Dundonnell: the planning minister approves;
the span
of the wind generator – length ...

Lops & splices
the wings
of Brolgas

XIV
Long-lived
Restricting the count
to juveniles

risks overlooking
a crash
in numbers of adult Brolgas

The severity
of dry times in the South West
unequalled

XV   (SW April 2015)
Driving into dark
off the curve of tableland
down to the Glenelg at Casterton
A Hummocky crouch
of bare hills:
massacre the foundation

XVI   (SW April 2015)
Windswept
wing swept
                winging it –
Swept away
        swept
                swept clean
'cleaning up':

The hills cleared —
  wing / wind
     swept
Wings
  swept away
    Gone
& the swamps

XVII
A net of fine branches
north of Heart Morass
the recently dead
old Forest Red Gums
casualties of irrigation:
salt raised by the MID

A fine filigree sculpture
in 2D flowers or stars
inside the metal body
of two Brolgas standing
on a bank above Mawley Rd:
last in Gippsland on a front door

XVIII After 'Brolga' serigraph (silk screen) by Ray Thomas c2000
A long-necked turtle swims
under the wing
of the leaping Brolga
as it steps and turns
to encounter
in freshwater
the reflection of many
flocking
to lagoons and marshes
across the Gippsland Plains

100 years ago

Calling
Ele! Ele! Eleocharis:
food for all its absent kin

XIX
How far can salt rise?
Sucked up by waters
departing for Melbourne

& half a billion
in annual currency
generated by dairy cows

Irreversible changes:
9000 ha of freshwater wetlands
rimmed Lake Wellington

The last freshwater wetland
a contaminated Common

XX
In the South West
in our children's lifetime
in *memorium*: Brolgas

PART THREE
GIBSON'S FOLLY

Gibson's Folly (Tambo River)
'Treat with *Euphrasia* bad memory and vertigo'

Gibson's Folly -

Earth Moving: the precipitous track descends to Wilga portal
and the Tambo

Purple Eyebright ringed around closely
in heathy dry forest
lilac, pink or white
 'it comes and goes'
but when it's gone, gladness
goes with it
the yellow spot behind the lower lobe
a guide to pollinating insects

Rock

Ore
Base metals
Copper & zinc:
The Wilga and Currawong
        massive sulphide deposits are hosted
                within deformed Upper Silurian volcanics
                        and sediments of the Gibsons Folly Formation
Other prospects: Dogwood, Mopoke, Big Hand, Banksia, Peppermint, Boxer
And Nameless
But Bigfoot may bear   GOLD
                    the richest   of   all

High Noon

The Waxlip Anomaly — a magnetic high at 12000N 15300E on the Wilga Grid
Tested by diamond drill *but no significant mineralisation was intersected*

Waxlip Spur, site of the old Benambra mine processing plant, an acid seep
runs down to the Tambo River & high flows shall dilute the heavy metals

43 species of orchids were discovered in the area including the Purple Waxlip
Glossodia major which forms no roots and depends upon mycorrizal fungi
   for nutrition

I run up the bare clay spur to the helipad with a view beyond the failed
   revegetation
into rugged country from Mt Tambo to the Nunniong escarpment

Wilga Spring

Beside the Tambo a natural spring issuing sulphides is a blind
for heavy metal seepage from the tailings dam on Straight Creek upstream

The small town of Swift's Creek draws off its water supply 30 kilometres
   down river

Horse

Riding with Gibson via the Bundara
Up through Charlie Mac's to the Bogongs
To lay down salt in trap-yards
Under the dappled sunlight of snow gums
Late spring snowdrifts and dark shadows
Replicate the flanks of piebald horses
                  *

Leaping the shallow stream
At the base of the tailings dam spillway
Last remnant of the rarest swamp
Sphagnum moss, Strawberry Buttercups
Sun Orchids and Bluebells
Trampled by hooves 'gone feral' across the Alps

SPZ 633

Blue-tongue Greenhood and sprawl of Knawel
at the foot of the dam wall -
                              in their own zone

rare companions among *Sphagnum* moss:
Montane Grass-trigger plant alongside Dusky Violet

when the dam wall is raised twice the height:
                              ' they were so elusive'

Mountain Banksia

High on the dry ridge
cylindrical yellow flowers of *Banksia canei*
                                        nectar
                                                licked
                                                        by
Eastern Pygmy Possums and Feathertail Gliders
and honeyeaters chasing *Grevillia*, *Corea* and *Callistemon* and thirteen
species of eucalypt around the slopes all year
                                        over
                                                look
the turquoise dam waters:
700,000 tonnes of

In the steep headwaters valley soon to be flooded more deeply

mine tailings: copper, zinc, cadmium, lead, arsenic, manganese, antimony
lying under

absence of euphrasey, blue-tongue, sprawling, and all those precious others
viol-ate

under dam waters *Sphagnum cristatum* and manifold springs along the
creek bed

the dam leaks
down through rock,
another 7 million tonnes
to be dumped, vertigo
in

Lake St Barbara:

by her name
poisonous waters
are rendered innocuous

PART FOUR
REMNANTS

Remnants
Gippsland Red Gum Plains

I. Yeerung Bush Reserve

A grey downy bird hops down the Yertchuk to look at me as I climb through the wire fence on the boundary of the badlands into Yeerung Reserve. She hops up and down the tree as if tapping on my heart, lightly. A female Golden Whistler. I'm here, she says, despite the eroded gulch of Fiddlers Creek as it re-enters dry farmland. Yertchuk and Red Gums shelter the shady interior of the tiny reserve. I could walk from one side to the other through patches of Kangaroo Grass and Wallaby Grass in ten minutes if I moved swiftly but I don't. The chain-of-ponds creek slows down in the reserve allowing creatures to sit and rest, to hide out from the heat, or to stay if they are able to live in small places. A Peregrine Falcon lifts off from the bank of a shadowy water hole, its strong yellow legs hanging straight down as it crosses the pool and rises through overhanging branches back out into the dissolving sun.

II. Stratford 113 Bush Reserve

Definition of remnant? Grassy woodland: 250 metres deep and 150 metres wide. The conservation officer had been enthusiastic: quality plains grassland divided in three for ecological fire management. I stop on the roadside verge looking into the small patch. Am I in the same place? On either side, sheep paddocks. In the southwest corner an old wooden gate falls half open. Under the regrowth Red Gums there's a single Clustered Everlasting plant with dry flower heads and nearby a clump of noxious St John's Wort. The long grasses are tinged by an orange glow from the 85,000 hectare Aberfeldy bushfire.

III. Briagalong Cemetery

A newly gravelled car park has been pushed in to the grassland.
Plastic flowers pile up in the dense long grass. A sign at the front gate
announces that the grassland is rare and threatened. Lines of blue
and white agapanthus demarcate the graveyard boundary. A deep
wheel rut cuts the earth at an angle, towards graves of a lesser faith
underneath a Blackwood tree, bisecting the hardened memory of rain.

IV. Briagalong Forest Reserve

In Angus McMillan's 'top paddock' all the Red Gums are the same
age: regrown from sleeper cutter days. The absence of large tree
hollows makes the forest almost uninhabitable. The forest block is
divided in two *—allow 35 minutes for a walk around the north block and
40 minutes for a walk around the south block —*each section may also be
traversed diagonally. Brayakaulung people had dwelt along the gully
in the northern block. The Scots did away with that. Someone has
built a bough shelter below the clay bank of a dam. Late afternoon
sunlight falls on the floor. I crouch down to look at the pattern of
leaves. Throughout the forest the sameness of trees is disturbing.

V. Boundary Rd

I pull up on the track to look north across the plains beyond Emu
Creek. A thousand sheep run down the slope towards me, swarming
over the dam wall. Encircling the brown water they stand on their
reflections. La Niña left East Gippsland six months ago.

VI. Tom's Creek Reserve

I cut across the flat to the eroded cliffs and follow the ruined creek
upstream. On a big bend the trampled sandbar is scattered with dry
cow pats. African Lovegrass has invaded the narrow strip of land
between the reserve fence and the edge of the gulch. I try to avoid

brushing the insidious fine seed heads. A few low trees planted by the *Red Gum Plains Recovery Project* have survived the rabbits. I look down into a still pool. A white Intermediate Egret stalks the reeds. At the junction of Tom's Creek and Emu Creek dark green Trees of Heaven have spread to the edge of the bank above a Cumbungi waterhole. Further west over the curve of bare paddocks, two white headstones from colonial times catch the afternoon light. The sign at Emu Creek ford acknowledges *Good Neighbours*.

VII. Meerlieu – Lindenow South Rd

For eighteen months it rained. Waterholes, lagoons and creeks re-appeared across the Gippsland Plains. Like the gradual revelation of an image from the dark water of a photographer's tank. Old routes and campsites along streamlines could be seen. Isolated ancient Red Gums stood at the edge of waterholes again. Crakes and rails crossed the road to wetlands. The sky was re-inhabited by birds. Thousands of ibis flew in formations over the Lindenow flats. Flocks of seed eating finches moved through the grasses and brightly coloured rosellas searched roadside trees for nesting hollows. Then it stopped raining.

VIII. Blond Bay Wildlife Reserve

Hog deer hunting season hasn't yet begun. Four-wheel drive tracks cut deep into the steep dunes. Romawi Run cleared for Black Wattle bark and burnt continually until moving sands shifted inland in the late 1950s. At the northern end of the reserve a few Red Gums wait together under the wide slope of cleared land running all the way down to Lake Victoria. At Waddy Point, waves lap mussel shells, beer cans and a discarded nappy under old Saw Banksias.

IX. Meerlieu 115 Bush Reserve

Last of the locals: big old Red Gums lean over the unused road leading into the bush reserve. I dance north over the old dunes through strappy Lomandra, bracken and White Stringybarks catching the Pleistocene wind as it blows down into a dune swale and up over the next sandhill: no Red Gums. Stands of grey-blue Mealy Stringybarks float in blue pools above the bracken. On the northern boundary, three Red Gums look out over cleared land moving with kangaroos. At dusk the unspoken knowledge is the thump of a Swamp Wallaby hit by a car in the gully as it crosses the road to the only adjacent bush.

X. Stratford Highway Park

So rare to see an un-trampled waterhole on the plains! Grassy woodland comes down to the shore. An island of white waterlilies floats in the lagoon dammed in the 19th century to refill steam locomotives: 'the usefulness of the useless'. A Black-fronted Dotterel drops in for a visit. Throughout the old railway reserve young Red Gums reclaim the gravel pit.

XI. Billabong Flora and Fauna Reserve

In sand dune country the dry billabong has shrunk inside a circumference of encroaching burgan. The track is overgrown and steel posts mark the rapid progress of burgan towards the prostrate strawberry leaves of endangered Dwarf Kerrawang trailing branches in spring bearing pink hairy star-shaped flowers by the edge of the lagoon where 'cattle once wallowed like water buffalo' colonies of rabbits now graze.

XII. Billabong West Reserve

Plume Grass, Wallaby Grass and Black She-oaks: the land is so much happier here under the spacious Red Gums. What remains alludes to the unseen: tree shadows, white fluff of cockatoo feathers suspended in long grass, and the ghost of a vast Red Gum forest.

XIII. Maffra Cemetery

Where: 'the unmown grass between two tombstones'? Neatly partitioned into quadrants belonging to their church, the dead take precedence over the living. The rare grassland that had survived 180 years of European occupation in a narrow strip beyond the protected native vegetation signs has been slashed down to dirt and the earth scraped smooth as a granite tomb.

XIV. Bush Family Reserve, Meerlieu, TFN

We *Spring into Nature* expecting to find the old forest: instead a sandy track winds through 80 year-old re-generating Red Gums. We cast about for a few huge stumps among the thousands of slender trees. Further off in the bush a group of people are gathered around the conservation officer listening to a talk on thinning trials being conducted by Trust for Nature in an attempt to re-create the original grassy woodland. Bracken from a history of hot burns covers the reserve. Burgan, signal of the land's ill-treatment, is massing in an adjoining block. Along a sand ridge, Milkmaids and Bulbine Lilies flower inside small fenced plots beyond the reach of wallabies. Beginning from so little, is the determination to celebrate admirable or naive?

XV. Friars Reserve

The heart of the block has been ripped out: White Stringybarks
logged and Saw Banksias burnt: broken limbs and black nobbly cones
against the sky. I follow kangaroo tracks through thick burgan into the
glare of the late afternoon sun. To the south and west in the distance
a boundary fringe of trees. Over the sandy rise an isolated grove of tall
Peppermints and Apple Box creates a refuge not to be disregarded for
the raucous flight home by eight gentle Gang Gangs.

XVI. Perry River

From Boney Point —
Name born of violence —
Down the green Avon
To Lake Wellington we paddle

A hog deer huntress
Comes down to the Perry
To threaten us away from her land
And Americans hunting from hides

In another world my friend asks:
What would we be poaching?
Paddling to look for a fern forest
In the last of the freshwater swamps

Out by Boney Point —
How unsafe the land became:
Poor, poor Perry
And the land that is undone.

PART FIVE
NOTES & SOURCES

I. Glide

Yellow-bellied Gliders *Petaurus australis*

Background

Eucalypt sap is a key food source for Yellow-bellied Gliders (YBG), which they obtain by chewing through the outer bark with their lower incisors to access the sugary nutrients flowing down the phloem of the inner bark. The incisions are frequently a distinctive V-shape but other patterns can also be observed. A family group (3-6 individuals) will use less than a dozen sap-feed trees within an exclusive home range of 30-65ha. Less than one per cent of all trees in a stand of forest may be sap-feed trees.

Phenology

Notes

Sap

Apple Box *(Eucalptus bridgesiana)* is one of the highly preferred sap-tree species in Mt Alfred State Forest.

Flow

Increased sap flow appears to be the defining characteristic for selection of sap-feed trees (Goldingay 1989). Yellow-bellied Gliders regularly make small incisions in selected trees to test for sap flow (Goldingay 2000).

Patchiness

YBG regularly test older currently unused sap-feed trees and older calloused over incisions may be re-opened some years after last use. In logged forests sap-feed trees may be protected in gullies as a consequence of retention of gully vegetation but this provides inadequate protection for YBG sap trees in general as most sap trees are located in mid-slope areas or on the ridges (Goldingay 2000:221). YBG sap-feed trees are not protected in Victorian logging coupes.

Eucalypt nectar is another key food source for YBG. However logging has destroyed the diversity of eucalypt species that occurred in old forest and which provided YBG with a succession of flowering (nectar bearing) species throughout the year.

"Honeydew is a sugar-rich liquid excreted by psyllids, coccids and aphids feeding on phloem sap. These insects are found on the upper branches of eucalypts, often under loose bark." (Henry and Craig 1984:334)

Manna is a white sugary substance formed from sap that is exuded at sites on the foliage and small branches damaged by sap-sucking insects. This may occur when new leaves are produced on eucalypts during periods of active growth. (Kavanagh1987:381).

Decorticating

Splitting the bark ribbons	Kavanagh 1987:372
They opened the hanging	Henry & Craig 1984:333

Timing of reproduction is affected by seasonal food patterns and availability. YBG females have a high requirement for protein (provided by arthropods) at birth of young and during late lactation; and similarly young gliders when first foraging independently (Goldingay & Kavanagh1990).

References

Goldingay, R.L., 1989. The behavioural ecology of the gliding marsupial, *Petaurus australis* PhD Thesis, Department of Biology, University of Wollongong http://ro.uow.edu.au/theses/1077

Goldingay, R.L., 2000. Use of sap trees by the Yellow-bellied Glider in the Shoalhaven region of New South Wales. *Wildlife Research*, 2000, 27, 217-222

Goldingay, R.L. & Kavanagh, R.P., 1990. Socioecology of the Yellow-bellied Glider *Petaurus australis*, at Waratah Creek, NSW. *Aust. J. Zool.*, 1990, 38, 327-41

Goldingay, R.L. & Kavanagh, R.P., 1991. The Yellow-bellied Glider: a review of its ecology and management consideration. Pages 365-75 *in* Conservation of Australia's Forest Fauna, ed. D. Lunney. Royal Zoological Society of NSW, Mossman, 1991.

Henry, S.R. & Craig, S.A., 1984. Diet, Ranging Behaviour and Social organisation of the Yellow-bellied Glider (*Petaurus australis* Shaw) in Victoria. Pages 331-41*in* Possums and Gliders, ed. A.P. Smith and I.D. Hume, Australian Mammal Society, Sydney, 1984, Ch. 31.

Kavanagh, R.P., 1987. Forest Phenology and its Effect on Foraging behaviour and

Selection of habitat by the Yellow-bellied Glider, *Petaurus australis* Shaw. *Aust. Wildl. Res.*, 1987, 14, 371-84

Lindenmayer, D., 2002. Gliders of Australia. UNSW Press, Sydney.

Wilson, J., 2003. Flowering Ecology of a Box-Ironbark *Eucalyptus* Community. PhD Thesis (May 2002) School of Ecology and Environment, Deakin University. https://dro.deakin.edu.au/eserv/DU:30023163/wilson-floweringecology-2003.pdf

Woodcut

Notes

Field observations are from Mt Alfred State Forest in Gippsland Forest Management Area & Errinundra Plateau in East Gippsland Forest Management Area.

YBG sap-feed trees may become elaborately carved from incisions made by gliders over many years.

YBG preferred sap-feed trees in Gippsland foothill forests include: Mountain Grey Gum: *Eucalyptus cypellocarpa*, (smooth barked); Apple Box: *E. bridgesiana* (rough barked);

& Messsmate: *E. obliqua* (rough barked).

Sivertop: *E. Sibieri* is not used by YBG as a sap tree.

Although YBG frequently use Apple Box as a sap-feed tree the species is not included in VicForests re-seeding of logging coupes after clear-felling.

Flight paths

Notes

Yellow-bellied Glider sap-feed trees may occur in clumps or groves but these are sparsely distributed across the landscape. Sap feed-trees are not protected from planned burns or clear-fell logging. Baldhills Creek Tk (Mitchell River National Park), Wattle Creek Tk, Stony Creek and Watts Creek areas are all scheduled for burning within the next two years; the Watts Creek Tk area is also scheduled to be logged in the near future.

Greater Glider (*Petauroides volans*)

Background

The Greater Glider was one of the most common arboreal mammals found in eucalypt forests of the Great Dividing Range until relatively recently (1990s). In 2020 the three populations of Greater Glider, southern, central and northern, were identified as separate species. The Southern Greater Glider, which retained the name *Petauroides volans*, inhabits the forests of East Gippsland.

In May 2016 the Greater Glider was listed as vulnerable to extinction under the national Environment Protection and Biodiversity Conservation Act (1999) due to a significant decline in the population. In June 2017 it was listed as threatened under Victoria's Flora and Fauna Guarantee Act (1988). Loss of old forest habitat (including hollow-bearing trees) due to logging is a key cause of the species' decline. Individual Greater Gliders may use more than a dozen different hollows for denning. According to the FFG Greater Glider Action Statement (December 2019) VicForests are only required to retain 40% of the basal timber area of a logging coupe if 5 or more GG are recorded within 1km.

Whaling

Notes

Greater Gliders show a strong attachment to their home range (only 1-2 ha) and when displaced by clear-fell logging do not migrate into other areas of standing forest. Whilst gliders are usually not killed by tree fall most of them will die within a week due to exposure or predators. The few gliders that do survive are those inhabiting a home range that is not entirely destroyed and which extended outside the coupe boundary.

The patagium (gliding membrane) of Greater Gliders, unlike most other gliders, extends only to the elbow not the wrist of its forelimbs so when gliding it flexes the elbow and draws its paws up under the chin. Greater Gliders feed on the young leaves and buds of a few Eucalypt species which contain relatively high concentrations of nitrogen (and phosphorous) and low concentration of ligno-cellulose (fibre).

In Victoria Narrow-leaved Peppermint (*E.radiata*) is widely preferred. Other Eucalypt species include White Stringybark (*E.globoidea*), Brown Barrel (*E.fastigata*) and Manna Gum (*E.viminalis*) and Mountain Grey Gum (*E.cypellocarpa*). Mistletoe leaves are also consumed.

In the Gippsland foothill forests Greater Gliders prefer mixed old growth forest of Mountain Grey Gum (*E. cypellocarpa*) and Messmate (*E.obliqua*) which readily form hollows as well as Narrow-leaved Peppermint and White Stingybark for their food.

Sivertop (*Eucalyptus seiberi*) which is commonly grown by VicForests in native hardwood plantations after the original mixed forest is clear felled is one of the least preferred tree species for Greater Gliders as it low in nitrogen and forms few hollows.

Selective logging carried out from the 1950s and extensive clear-fell logging since the 1990s has left very little old-growth forest in the Stony Ck and Wattle Ck catchments between Mt Alfred and the Mitchell River National Park 25kms to the west.

References

Kavanagh, R.P., 2000. Effects of variable-intensity logging and the influence of habitat variables on the distribution of the Greater Glider *Petauroides volans* in montane forest, southeastern New South Wales. *Pacific Conservation Biology* vol. 6:18-30.Surrey Beatty & Sons, Sydney.

Kavanagh, R.P. & Lambert, M. J., 1990. Food selection by the Greater Glider, Petauroides volans: Is Foliar Nitrogen a Determinant of Habitat Quality? *Aust.Wildl.Res*, 1990, 17, 285-99

Smith, A.P., 27 January 2010. Effects of logging on populations of the Greater Glider (*Petauroides volans*) and Yellow-bellied Glider (*Petaurus australis*) in Four Coupes at Brown Mountain, East Gippsland, Victoria. Expert Witness Report to the Supreme Court of Victoria, austeco Environmental Consultants, Elanora, QLD.

Tyndale-Biscoe, C.H. & Smith, R.F.C., 1969. Studies on the Marsupial Glider, *Schoinblates volans* (Kerr): III. Response to Habitat Destruction. *Journal of Animal Ecology*, Vol. 38, No 3 (Oct. 1969), 651-659.

Tyndale-Biscoe, C.H. & Calaby, J.H., 1975. Eucalypt Forest as Refuge for Wildlife. *Australian Forestry*, 38, 117-133

Horizontal

Notes

II. from Kavanagh & Wheeler 2004: 424

IV Only known breeding site of Giant Burrowing Frog in Victoria (as of 2019) is in Watts Creek (east branch). A Special Protection Zone to protect the GBF prevents logging in the immediate area.

V. Greater Gliders are usually dark grey-black with white underneath their chest and a long grey-black tail. However some are quite pale and their colour can be quite variable ranging from smoky-grey, mottled grey, grey back with cream head and tail, to cream all over.

References

Kavanagh, R.P. & Wheeler, R.J., 2004 Home-range of the greater glider *Petauraoides volans* in tall montane forest of southeastern New South Wales, and changes following logging. Pages 413-25 *in* The Biology of Aust Possums and Gliders, ed. by R.L. Goldingay and S.M. Jackson. Surrey Beatty & Sons, Chipping Norton.

Home Range

Notes

The Greater Glider has a home range area of between 1-2ha. They have a strong site attachment to their home range and when displaced by clear-felling will not migrate into adjacent forest. They generally do not survive longer than a week after felling of their habitat.

References

Department of Environment and Energy, 2016. 'Conservation Advice *Petauroides volans* Greater Glider'. Department of Environment and Energy, Australian Government, Canberra.
http://www.environment.gov.au/biodiversity/threatened/species/pubs/254-conservation-advice-05052016.pdf (Accessed 7.2.2017)

Henry, S.R., 1984. Social organisation of the Greater Glider (*Petauroides volans*) in Victoria.

Kavanagh, R.P. & Wheeler, R.J., 2004. Home-range of the greater glider *Petauroides volans* in tall montane forests of southeastern New South Wales, and changes following logging. Pages 413-25 *in* The Biology of Australian Possums and Gliders ed. by R.L. Goldingay and A.M. Jackson. Surrey Beatty & Sons, Chipping Norton. 2004.

Pages 221-28 *in* Possums and Gliders, ed. by A.P. Smith and I.D. Hume, Australian Mammal Society, Sydney, 1984.

Calculation
Notes

Scientific name *Petauroides volans*: flying rope-walker.

Individual Greater Gliders use numerous different den hollows. DBH: diameter at breast height.

'Habitat tree' refers to a tree protected from logging to 'provide habitat or future habitat for wildlife'. It may be living or dead and 'often contains hollows'. (Code of Practice, 2014). In Gippsland Forest Management Areas old living trees with a range of hollows are required to be prioritised as habitat trees but if these are absent or in insufficient numbers, trees that may develop hollows in 50 years are prioritised. Stags (broken dead trees) and younger smaller trees may be counted if larger living trees are absent.

Vic Forests' regeneration burns frequently destroy the retained habitat trees and understory vegetation.

References

DEPI 2014 Code of Practice for Timber Production 2014 Department of Environment and Primary Industry, Victoria.

DEPI 2014 Management Standards and Procedures for timber harvesting operations in Victoria's State Forests, 2014 Department of Environment and Primary Industry, Victoria.

Kavanagh, R.P. & Wheeler, R.J., 2004. "Home-range of the greater glider *Petauroides volans* in tall montane forests of southeastern New South wales, and changes following logging" pages 413-25 *in* The Biology of Australian Possums and Gliders ed by R.L. Goldingay and A.M. Jackson. Surrey Beatty & Sons, Chipping Norton. 2004.

Kehl, J. & Borsboom, A., "Home range, den tree use and activity patterns in the Greater Glider , Petauroides volans" pages 229-36 *in* Possums and Gliders, ed. By

A.P. Smith and I.D. Hume. Australian Mammal Society. Sydney, 1984

Kerle, A., 2001. "Possums: The Brushtails, Ringtails and Greater Glider", Aust Natural History Series, UNSW Press, Sydney.

Lindenmayer, D., 1992. "The Ecology and Habitat requirements of Arboreal Marsupials in the Montane Ash Forests of the Central Highlands of Victoria: summary of studies". VSP Internal report no.6 Department of Conservation and Environment, Kew, Victoria.

Smith, A.P., 27 January 2010. "Effects of logging on populations of the Greater glider (*Petauroides volans*) and Yellow-bellied Glider (*Petaurus australis*) in Four Coupes at Brown Mountain, East Gippsland, Victoria." Expert witness Report to the Supreme Court of Victoria, austeco Environmental Consultants, Elanora, QLD.

Sugar Glider (*Petaurus breviceps*)

Haulage
Notes
Research shows that Sugar Glider populations fail to recover within eight years after clear fell logging of their habitat.

References
Kavanagh, R.P. & Webb, G.A., 1998. Effects of variable-intensity logging on mammals, reptiles and amphibians at Waratah Creek, southeastern New South Wales. *Pacific Conservation Biology*, Vol 4:326-47. Surrey Beatty & Sons, Sydney, 1998

Fireflies
Notes
Black wattle (*Acacia mearnsii*).

The territorial call of a Sooty Owl sounds like the whistle of a bomb dropping.

References
Henry, S.R. & Suckling, G.C., 1984. A review of the Ecology of the Sugar Glider. Pages 355-58 *in* Possums and Gliders, ed. By A.P. Smith and I.D. Hume, Australian Mammal Society, Sydney, 1984.

Lindenmayer, D., 2002. Gliders of Australia: Australian Natural History Series.

UNSW Press, Sydney.

Smith, A.P., 1982. Diet and Feeding Strategies of the Marsupial Sugar Glider in Temperate Australia. *Journal of Animal Ecology* (1982), 51, 149-166.

Van der Ree, R., Ward, S.J. & Handasyde, K.A., 2004. Distribution and conservation status of possums and gliders in Victoria. Pages 91-110 *in* The Biology of Australian Possums and Gliders, ed. by R.L. Goldingay & S.M.Jackson. Surrey Beatty & Sons, Chipping Norton, 2004.

Windsucking

Notes

Sugar Gliders are one of key vertebrate pollinators of Saw Banksia.

Blue Box or Round-leaved Box (*Eucalyptus baueriana*) is a Eucalypt found in rare Limestone Box Forest.

An area in Lake Tyers State Park containing Limestone Box Forest and Lowland Banksia Forest that has remained unburned for 60 years was scheduled by Forest Fire Management Victoria to be burnt in autumn 2017 but the planned burn (Nelson Rd – Nowa Nowa) was deferred following protests by locals.

References

Copland, B.J. & Whelan, R.J., 1989. Seasonal Variation in Flowering Intensity and Pollination Limitation of Fruit Set in Four Co-occurring Banksia Species. *Journal of Ecology*, Vol 27, No.2 (June 1989), pp. 509-523

Smith, A.P., 1982. Diet and Feeding Strategies of the Marsupial Sugar Glider in Temperate Australia. *Journal of Animal Ecology*, Vol. 51, No.1 (Feb. 1982), pp.149-166

Feathertail Glider (*Acrobates pygmaeus*)

Ash

Notes

Location - Flaggy Ck tributary, Melwood School Rd coupe 735-505-0001, Mt Alfred State Forest, Tambo FMA.

Feathertail Gliders are tiny, weighing 10-14 grams, and live in groups of

2-29 individuals. Diet includes arthropods, nectar, honeydew, pollen, seeds and fruit. Prefers older forests with hollow bearing trees for shelter and specialised food resources. A key requirement is trees with an abundance of loose bark (eg. *E. ovata*, *E. cypellocarpa*, *E. viminalis*) which provide opportunity to forage for arthropods.

The Feathertail Glider is presumed to be common but actual population numbers are unknown as it is so small it is rarely seen when spotlighting consequently few studies have been conducted.

Sunshine wattle (*Acacia terminalis*).

Blue Oliveberry (*Elaeocarpus reticulatus*)

References

Goldingay, R.L. and Eyre, T.J., 2004. Structural habitat preferences of the feathertail glider on the mid-north coast of New South Wales. Pages 290-97 *in* The Biology of Australian Possums and Gliders, ed. by R.L. Goldingay and S.M. Jackson. Surrey Beatty & Sons, Chipping Norton, 2004.

Goldingay, R.L. and Kavanagh, R.P., 1995. Foraging Behaviour and Habitat Use of the Feathertail Glider (*Acrobates pygmaeus*) at Waratah Creek, New South Wales. *Wildlife Research*, 1995, 22, 457-70.

Harris, J.M. and Maloney, K.S., 2006. Annotated records of the feathertail glider, acrobates pygmaeus, from the Victorian Naturalist. *The Victorian Naturalist*, 123 (3), 157-165.

Lindenmayer, D., 2002. Gliders of Australia: a natural history. UNSW Press, Sydney.

Squirrel glider (*Petaurus norfolcensis*)

Extinction

Notes

Epigraph from "The Earthdom of a Bird" in *The Trees: selected poems 1967-2004* by Eugenio Montale, translated by Peter Boyle. Salt Publishing, Cambridge UK & Applecross WA, 2004.

The Squirrel Glider *Petaurus norfolcensis* is listed as endangered in Victoria. It is now extinct in Gippsland although it was present at the time of European settlement. The Squirrel Glider persists in northern and central

Victoria where it inhabits mature mixed Eucalypt woodland with an understory of Acacia species particularly *A. mearnsii* and *A. dealbata*. The Gippsland Red Gum plains grassy woodlands and drier mixed forests of the lowland foothills occurring on fertile soils have been extensively cleared for agriculture. Many small mammal species have now disappeared from the region. Of 28 small mammal species that were identified in Sooty Owl roost sites in the Gippsland foothills in sub-fossil deposits, indicating they were present at the time of European settlement, only 10 species were detected in the contemporary Sooty Owl diet.

Squirrel Glider bones have been found in sub-fossil deposits in Eastern Quoll dens and owl roost sites in caves at Murrindal near Buchan and in Sooty owl roost sites in rock shelters at Iguana Ck and Friday Ck, foothill tributaries of the Mitchell River.

The Squirrel Glider is very similar in appearance to the Sugar Glider but is larger with a bushier tail.

The Eastern Quoll is now probably extinct on mainland Australia.

References

Ahern, L. & van der Ree, R., 2003. Squirrel Glider *Petaurus norfolcensis,* Action Statement no. 166, Flora and Fauna Guarantee Act 1988, prepared for Department of Sustainability and Environment, DSE Victoria.

Bilney, R. J., Cooke, R. & White, J. G., 2010. Underestimated and severe: Small mammal decline from the forests of south-eastern Australia since European settlement, as revealed by a top-order predator. *Biological Conservation* 143 (2010)52-59.

Van der Ree, R.,Ward, S.J. and Handasyde, K.A., 2004. Distribution and conservation status of possums and gliders in Victoria. Pages 91-110 *in* The Biology of Australian Possums and Gliders, ed. by R.L. Goldingay and S.M. Jackson. Surrey Beatty & Sons, Chipping Norton, 2004.

Wakefield, N.A., 1960a. Recent mammal bones in the Buchan district − 1. *The Victorian Naturalist* 77: 164-178.

Wakefield, N.A., 1960a. Recent mammal bones in the Buchan district − 2. *The Victorian Naturalist* 77:227-240.

Night Country

Notes

2. Title from Bandt, 2001: 4

The five major clans of the Gunaikurnai nation: Brabralung, Brataualung, Brayakaulung, Krauatungalung and Tatungalung.

Phrase 'taxanomic subtleties', from Mansergh & Hercus, 1981:110

Mansergh and Hercus list the species name and common name of the four glider species currently extant in Gippsland that they consider refer to the 19th century English vernacular names and the corresponding Gunaikurnai words. The four glider species in order of decreasing size are the Greater Glider (*Petauroides volans*), Yellow-bellied Glider (*Petaurus autralis*), Sugar Glider (*Petaurus breviceps*) and Feathertail Glider (*Acrobates pygmaeus*).

It's possible that one or more of the Gunaikurnai words translated as 'squirrel' in the English vernacular by colonial recorders may have referred to the Squirrel Glider (*Petaurus norfolcensis*), which is larger than the Sugar Glider and was present in Gippsland at the time of European invasion but is now regionally extinct.

References

Bandt, R., 2001. Hearing Australian Identity: Sites as acoustic spaces, an audible polyphony. Australian Sound Design Project, The Australian Centre, University of Melbourne. http://www.sounddesign.unimelb.edu.au/site/NationPaper/NationPaper.html

Belfrage, J., 1994. The Great Australian Silence: Inside acoustic space. Australian Sound Design Project, University of Melbourne.
http://www.sounddesign.unimelb.edu.au/site/papers/AusSilence.html

Mansergh, I. and Hercus, L.A., 1981. An Aboriginal Vocabulary of the Fauna of Gippsland. *Memoirs of the National Museum Victoria*, No. 42.

Postscript: The 2019-20 summer bushfires burnt more than one million hectares of forest in East Gippsland. However VicForests pre-fire logging plans remain in place and the state-owned company approved two additional logging schedules in July and December 2020.

II. Brolga

Background

The Brolga (*Grus rubicunda*) is listed as threatened under the Victorian Flora and Fauna Guarantee Act 1988, (Action Statement no.119).

Brolgas were formerly widely distributed across south-eastern Australia. The species was once commonly recorded around Melbourne, Gippsland and North-eastern Victoria.

In Victoria Brolgas are now only found in the South West (Western District), the Northern Plains and adjacent areas of the Murray River.

In Gippsland Brolgas were common around the Sale area (adjacent to Lake Wellington in the Gippsland Lakes) until the 1920's; the most recent record is from Lakes Entrance in 1944.

Currently the largest population in Victoria is found in the South West. Population estimates vary: 600-650 birds (DSE 2003 AS p2 based on Arnol *et al* 1984); 200-250 breeding pairs (GHCMA 2015); 449 birds were observed during the April 2015 count (SWIFFT 2016).

A much smaller isolated population (approx 60-70) is found on the Northern Plains and adjacent parts of the Murray River however there has been no formal count for many years.

The draining of shallow freshwater wetlands used by Brolgas for nesting is the primary cause of their decline as well as predation of young and eggs by foxes.

A permanent entrance to the Gippsland Lakes was constructed in 1889 consequently the once freshwater to brackish lakes became increasingly saline. The Victorian Department of Sustainability and Environment approved further deepening of the entrance in 2008 and 2011.

Notes

Location shifts between Gippsland, and South Western Victoria indicated by (SW).

Research was undertaken on Gunaikurnai, Djab Wurrung, Jardwadjali and Baundig countries.

I. The Highland Brigade was a band of Scottish colonists including Angus

MacMillan, responsible for massacres of the Gunaikurnai in Gippsland in the 1840's.

II. *Exploring the Gippsland Lakes in 1882*, Paynesville Maritime Museum 2010, p10, 11.

Ramahyuck Aboriginal Mission (1862 -1908) was located on higher ground overlooking Clydebank Morass on the Avon River near its entrance into Lake Wellington. The Mission station was only a few kilometres to the west across the Perry River from Strathfieldsaye homestead and Swell Point Picnic Ground.

Lake Wellington is the westernmost lake of the Gippsland Lakes system.

III. Victorian Minister for Agriculture Jaala Pulford, on the advice of the Game Management Authority, refused to close Bullrush Swamp to duck hunters in March 2015. The Minister declared the adjacent Krause Swamp closed to hunting to provide a refuge for Brolgas although Krause Swamp had already been dry for some months.

See http://abc.net.au/news/2015-03-21/threatened-brolgas-risk-being-caught-in-duck-hunting-crossfire/6337302 (accessed 31.3.2105)

The Hamilton Field Naturalists Club has been lobbying the Victorian Government since 2005 to restore the sanctuary status of Lake Linlithgow and adjacent Bullrush Swamp which was overturned in the 1975 revision of the Wildlife Act.

IV. "the heart of Gippsland" Tyers 1844 ref Gippsland Heritage Journal Vol 1, No1 (1986) reproduced in Wise and Hurst 2011p6;

"heart carved in a tree": Montgomery, E., (1916)2003 p8;

"heart carved on a tree...and a heart also cut in the ground": Harrison in Leslie and Cowie 1973, p44;

"two hearts": Mrs Montgomery-Stubbs Family History, http://stubbs familyhistory.files.wordpress.com/2011/02/mrs-montgomery1.docx (accessed 25.6.2015)

"heart shaped where it joined the big waterhole" W.D. Leslie *Gippsland Times* 16 Oct 1919 in Wise and Hurst 2011 Foreward;

"aboriginal 'corroboree' ground ... figures marked out on the ground, one of which was heart shaped" Chas Lucas (arrived Gippsland Feb.1844) in Wise and Hurst 2011, p6 "numerous and hostile" George Campbell Curlewis quoted in Mrs Montgomery-Stubbs Family History http://stubbsfamilyhistory.files. wordpress.com/2011/02/mrs-montgomery1.docx (accessed 25.6.15)

"the whitemen heartless" G.A. Robinson 3 June 1841 quoted in Clark 1995, p 31.

V. Montgomery (1916) 2003, p 15,16

VI. Paynesville Maritime Museum, 2010 p10. *Phragmites sp* : Common rush

VII. Tatungalung clan of Gunaikurnai nation. Tatungalung country includes the islands and waterways of the Gippsland Lakes and fringing wetlands.

VIII & IX. In the south west of Victoria 79% of shallow freshwater marshes, which are the preferred breeding wetlands for Brolgas, have been drained for agriculture. The deep freshwater marshes, which Brolgas flock to during the drier non-breeding months of summer and autumn, have been reduced in extent by 66% (DSE 2003:2).

XII. *The Illustrated Australian News*, n.d, "Ramahyuck, Aboriginal Mission Station, Lake Wellington, Gipps Land", http://nla.gov.au/nla.news-page 5732718 (accessed 19.6.2015)

Gippsland Times, 1925, "Stocking the Rivers with Yearling Trout", 18 June 1925, p2, http://nla.gov.au/nla.news-article62569677 (accessed 30.6.2015.)

The construction of a permanent entrance to the Gippsland Lakes in 1889 and dredging since 2008 to maintain the entrance at greater depth has increased the tidal speed, causing a greater volume of seawater to enter the lakes and the once freshwater fringing wetlands.

XIII. The Victorian Planning Minister Richard Wynne approved Trustpower's Dundonnell wind farm project on7 February 2016. The Environmental Effects Statement reported that 52 Brolga flocking sites have been recorded in the radius (approx 10km) of the wind farm (Cumming 2016).

XIV. Since the April 2015 the Department of Environmental Land Water and Planning (DELWP) has only counted juvenile Brolgas in its annual count not the total population as had been the case for a number of years previously. This is despite the commitment detailed in the Brolga Action Statement (DSE 2003:5)

XV. The Hummocks, near Wando Vale north of Casterton, referred to as the Fighting Hills following the massacre of *Jardwadjali* people by the Whyte bros. in March 1840 (Clark 1995:144).

XVII. MID: the Macalister Irrigation District covers an area of 53,000 ha from Lake Glenmaggie to near Sale

XVIII. The tubers of *Eleocharis sp*, Spike Rush, were a major food source for Brolgas.

XIX. Increased diversions of freshwater from the rivers that flowed into Lake Wellington, including the construction of the Thompson Dam to supply water to Melbourne (approx. 40% of requirements) in the late 1970's and for agriculture and industrial use (80% of La Trobe Valley power stations' requirements), has exacerbated the increasing salinity of Lake Wellington and surrounding wetlands caused by a combination of marine inflows and saline groundwater from land clearing and irrigation. Lake Wellington crossed the threshold to a permanently saline ecosystem in the late 1960's, prior to this time dense beds of the freshwater submerged plant *Vallisneria australis* dominated the lake vegetation (Tilleard et al 2009, p41).

"Sale Common is the only true remaining freshwater wetland in the entire system", (Tilleard & Ladson, 2010:54)

Brolga: *kurakan* (Gunaikurnai), (Mansergh and Hercus, 1981)

XX. Quotation from Glenelg Hopkins Catchment Management Authority website, Wetlands page: http://www.ghcma.vic.gov.au/water/wetlands (accessed 26.5.2015).

References:

Arnol, J.D., White, D.M., and Hastings, I., 1984, *Management of the Brolga (Grus rubicundus) in Victoria*, Resources and Planning Branch, Technical Report Series no.6, Fisheries and Wildlife Service, Department of Conservation, Forests and Lands

Bird, R., 2011 *The Hamilton region of south western Victoria: a historical perspective of landscape, settlement and impacts on Aborigine occupants, flora and fauna*, P.R. Bird Publisher, Hamilton, Victoria.

Brolga FAQ 2 (2013) Australian Crane Network http://www.ozcranes.net/species/brolga_2.html (accessed 26.5.2015)

Casanova, M.T., 2012, "Does cereal crop agriculture in dry swamps damage aquatic plant communities?" *Aquatic Botany*, 103, (2012): 54-59.

Clark, I.D., 1995 *Scars in the Landscape: a register of massacre sites in Western Victoria, 1803-1859*, Report Series, Australian Institute of Aboriginal and Torres Strait Islander Studies, Canberra

Corrick, A.H., and Norman, F.I., 1980 "Wetlands and Waterbirds of the Snowy River and Gippsland Lakes Catchment", *Proc, Royal Soc. of Vict.* 91:1-15

Cumming, H., 2016 *Brolgas for the future* http://www.change.org/p/richard-protect-brolga-habitat-in-southwest-victoria-now (accessed 21.3.2016)

DSE 2003 Action Statement no 119, Brolga (*Grus rubicunda*) Flora and Fauna Guarantee Act 1988

Garnet, D., 1944 'Gippsland Notes' in Bird Observers' Club *Monthly Notes* January 1944, Bird Observers' Club, Melbourne

Gippsland Times, 1946 "Gippsland lakes Fifty Years Ago: Support for Closing the Entrance", 3 January 1946, p3 http://nla.gov.au/nla.news-article5417113 (accessed 30.9.2013)

Glenelg Hopkins Catchment Management Authority – GHCMA, Wetlands at http://www.ghcma.vic.gov.au/water/wetlands/ (accessed 26.5.15)

Herring, M., 2014 *Dancing Brolgas, Part 1, A national icon: trouble in the south*, http://www.ozcranes.net/species/matt1_1.html (accessed 14.3.2014)

Hutchinson, J. *The Gippsland Lakes as a drought refuge for nomadic birds*, http://avithera.blogspot.com.au (accessed 18.8. 2015)

Leslie, J.W. and Cowie, H.C., (eds.) 1973, *The Wind Still Blows... Extracts from the Diaries of Rev. W.S. Login, Mrs. H. Harrison, Mrs. W. Montgomery*, Gippsland Times Printing Service, Sale

Lyndon, E., 1993, *Door to the Forest: collected stories from one of nature's lifelong friends*, South Gippsland Conservation Society Inc Environment Centre, Inverloch, Victoria

Mansergh, I. and Hercus, L.A., 1981, *An Aboriginal Vocabulary of the Fauna of Gippsland*, Memoirs of the National Museum of Victoria, No. 42, 1981.

Michie, F., 2015 *Threatened brolgas risk being caught in duck hunting crossfire: environmentalists*, http://abc.net.au/news/2015-03-21/threatened-brolgas-risk-being-caught-in-duck-hunting-crossfire/6337302 (accessed 31.3.2015.)

Montgomery, E., (1916) 2003 *Mrs Montgomery's life in Gippsland*, The Stratford and District Historical Society Inc, Stratford.

Parks Victoria, 2008 *Lake Wellington Wetlands, Management Plan November 2008*, Parks Victoria, Melbourne

Paynesville Maritime Museum, 2010 *Exploring the Gippsland Lakes in 1882*, facsimile of *The Tourist's and Sportsman's Guide to the Gippsland Lakes and Surrounding Country*, compiled by J. Blackwood Howie for the Lakes Navigation Company c. 1882

Robinson, G. A., 1841 *The Journals of George Augustus Robinson, Chief Protector, Port Phillip Aboriginal Protectorate, Volume Two: 1 October 1840-31 August 1841*, ed. Ian D. Clark, Heritage Matters Melbourne 1998

Robinson, G.A., 1844 *The Journals of George Augustus Robinson, Chief Protector, Port Phillip Aboriginal Protectorate, Volume Four: 1 January 1844- 24 October 1845*, ed. Ian D. Clark, Heritage Matters, Melbourne, 1998

SWIFFT State Wide Integrated Flora and Fauna Teams, 2016, *The South-West Victoria Brolga Research Project: Key Findings, Key research findings 2015*, http://www.swifft.net.au/cb_pages/key_findings.php (accessed 3.5.2016)

Tilleard, J.W. and Ladson, A.R., 2010, *Understanding the environmental water requirements of the Gippsland Lakes system, Stage 2, Input to the Gippsland Sustainable Water Strategy*, a report by Moroka Pty Ltd for the East and West Gippsland Catchment Management Authorities, April 2010, p 54 (Attachment 1:36)

Tilleard, J.W., O'Connor, N. and Boon, P.I., (2009) *Understanding the environmental water requirements of the Gippsland lakes system- scoping study*, report by Moroka Pty Ltd, Ecos Environmental Consulting and Dodo Environmental for the East and West Gippsland Catchment Management Authorities

Wheeler, R., 1949, 'Early Records – The Native Companion' in Bird Observers' Club *Monthly Notes*, October 1949, Bird Observers' Club, Melbourne

White, D.M., 1987, *The Status and Distribution of the Brolga in Victoria, Australia*, Proc. 1983 International Crane Workshop, pp 115-131

Wise, J. and Hirst, J., 2011 *The Heart of Gippsland: From 1831 to 1948*, Sale & District Family History Group Project, Sale

III. Gibson's Folly

Background

The Benambra mine is located on the headwaters of the Tambo River which flows into the Ramsar listed Gippsland Lakes. The Wilga ore body was mined by Denehurst from 1992-96. The tailings dam destroyed 90% of the largest and most unique example of a rare montane swamp ecological community. The company went into receivership in 1998 and abandoned the site, leaving behind a leaking tailings dam which the Victorian Department of Primary Industry remediated at a cost to the taxpayer of $6.9 million in

2006. Following the mine site rehabilitation the tailings dam was re-named Lake St Barbara, after the patron saint of miners. It is still leaking polluted water containing copper and zinc and other heavy metals through the dam wall embankment. The dam operates as a flow through system depending on rainfall.

In 2012 Independence Group proposed to develop the Stockman Mine project and re-open the Wilga mine and develop the Currawong mine. The company planned to expand the tailings dam to store up to an additional 7 million tonnes of toxic tailings. In the process the dam wall would be raised another 25 metres above the valley floor to a total height of nearly 45 metres and increase the surface area of the dam from 8.5 ha to approx 35 ha. Another section of the nationally endangered sphagnum swamp will be destroyed along with 320 *Banksia canei* and a number of other rare species also affected.

The Stockman Mine project Environmental Effects Statement was approved by the Victorian Minister for Planning Mathew Guy in Oct. 2014 and by the Commonwealth Minister for Environment Greg Hunt in Dec. 2014. The Stockman project was acquired by Washington H Soul Pattinson in December 2017.

Notes

SPZ – Special Protection Zone. Under current legislation mining is not excluded from these zones.

Rare & protected species in order of reference:

Purple Eyebright: *Euphrasia collina* subsp *muelleri*
Purple Waxlip: *Glossodia major*
Sphagnum moss: *Sphagnum cristatum*
Strawberry Buttercup: *Ranunculus collinus*
Kiandra (Blue tongue) Greenhood: *Pterostylis oreophila*
Spawling Knawel: *Scleranthus fasiculatus*
Montane Grass-trigger plant: *Stylidium montanum*
Dusky violet: *Viola fuscoviolacea*
Mountain Banksia: *Banksia canei*
Sun orchid: *Thelymitra* sp.

Other species: Bluebells: *Wahlenbergia* sp

IV. Remants

Background

Gippsland Red Gum Grassy Woodlands and Associated Native Grassland ecological community was listed as critically endangered under the federal Environment Protection and Biodiversity Conservation Act 1999 (EPBC Act) on 7.01.09. Extensive clearing of the Gippsland Plains has reduced the extent of Red Gum Grassy Woodland by 97%. Remnants are highly fragmented across the Plain and few large patches have survived. The grassland component has a total extent of only 30-60ha. *Commonwealth Listing Advice on Gippsland Red Gum (Eucalyptus teriticornis subsp. mediana) Grassy Woodland and Associated Native Grassland*, Threatened Species Scientific Committee, 2008. Available from: http://www.environment.gov.au/sprat (accessed 24.9.11)

Notes

II. "'The end of nature', Bill McKibbin calls the collapse of life-support systems into remnants." Geoff Park, *Ngā Uruora: the Groves of Life*, Wellington: Victoria University Press, 1995:300. Bill McKibbin, *The End of Nature*, London: Penguin, 1992.

IV Brayakaulung clan of the Gunaikurnai nation.

XI. 'People all know the usefulness of what is useful but they do not know the usefulness of the useless' Zhuang Zi, third century. BC, quoted by Simon Leys in *The Halls of Uselessness*, Melbourne: Black Inc. 2011: 399.

XIII. 'A patch of unmown grass between two tombstones may be the only place in all the country where the same plants grow, and in the same numbers, as grew in that place long before...' Gerald Murnane, *Inland*, Melbourne: Heinemann 1988:15

XIV. 'Extinction is usually the end point of a long process of depletion.' *Draft Fauna and Flora Guarantee Strategy: Conservation of Victoria's Biodiversity*, DSE: Victoria 1992. Cited in Neville Scarlett, 'The Plains Wanderer: The

Metaphorical Grassland – Museum, Ark or Life-boat'. *Indigenotes* 6(1)1993:2
Burgan (*Kunzea ericoides*) is a native species which grows rampantly
following land disturbance by fire, clearing, or over-grazing by stock.

Trust for Nature (TFN) was established in Victoria in 1972 as a not-for-
profit organisation to protect native flora and fauna on private land through
conservation covenants. The Trust also owns and manages some properties,
as well as purchasing to protect and then on-sell properties through its
Revolving Fund.

XVI Boney Point at the junction of the Avon River and Perry River is the site
of a massacre in 1840 of Gunaikurnai people by Gippsland colonists (Angus
MacMillan and the Highland Brigade).

Acknowledgements

Louise Crisp lives and writes on the unceded lands of the Brabralung people of the Gunaikurnai nation and pays her deep respects to their elders past, present and future.

Some of these poems or extracts have appeared in the *Australian Anthology of Prose Poetry* (Melbourne University Press, 2020), *Contemporary Australian Poetry* (Puncher & Wattman, 2016) and *Cordite Poetry Review*.

This book was written with support from the Australian Government through the Australia Council, its arts and funding advisory body, and the Victorian Government through Creative Victoria.